This Walker  Book belongs to:

....

....

To each and every EXPERT — to those parents, educators, chefs, nutritionists, pediatricians, nurses, and child-development specialists who read over and looked over our work, talked to us, taught us, and corrected us over and over again as we created this book for young children. We could not have created this book without you. THANK YOU! — R. H. H.

For Seamus
N. B. W.

First published 2014 by Walker Books Ltd
87 Vauxhall Walk, London SE11 5HJ

2 4 6 8 10 9 7 5 3 1

Text © 2014 Bee Productions, Inc.
Illustrations © 2014 Nadine Bernard Westcott

The right of Robie H. Harris and Nadine Bernard Westcott to be identified as author
and illustrator respectively of this work has been asserted by them in accordance
with the Copyright, Designs and Patents Act 1988

This book was typeset in Berkeley Old Style and Little Grog

Printed and bound in China

British Library Cataloguing in Publication Data:
a catalogue record for this book is available from the British Library

ISBN 978-1-4063-5803-2

www.walker.co.uk

What's So Yummy?

All About

Eating Well and Feeling Good

Robie H. Harris

illustrated by Nadine Bernard Westcott

WALKER BOOKS
AND SUBSIDIARIES

LONDON • BOSTON • SYDNEY • AUCKLAND

Everybody everywhere needs to eat and drink.

Hey, Gus, it's picnic day! And what I love about picnics is all the good food we get to eat. It's so yummy!

Babies, children and grown-ups all get hungry and thirsty many times a day. In the morning, when we wake up, we often feel hungry and thirsty. The food and drinks that go into our bodies at breakfast time fill us up and make our bodies feel good. They also give us the power to do all the things that we want and have to do during the day.

I've just eaten porridge and an orange. Now I feel strong! And ready to ride to the supermarket and the farmers' market.

I ate an egg, toast, strawberries and milk for breakfast. Now I'm wide-awake! And ready to ride to our city garden.

Families get their food and drinks at corner shops, supermarkets, grocery stores, food banks and farmers' markets. Some also grow food in their garden, in a community garden, or on their farm. Others grow a bit of food in a pot outside or in a window box at their flat or house.

Sometimes families go out to a restaurant, food stall or snack bar to have something to eat and drink.

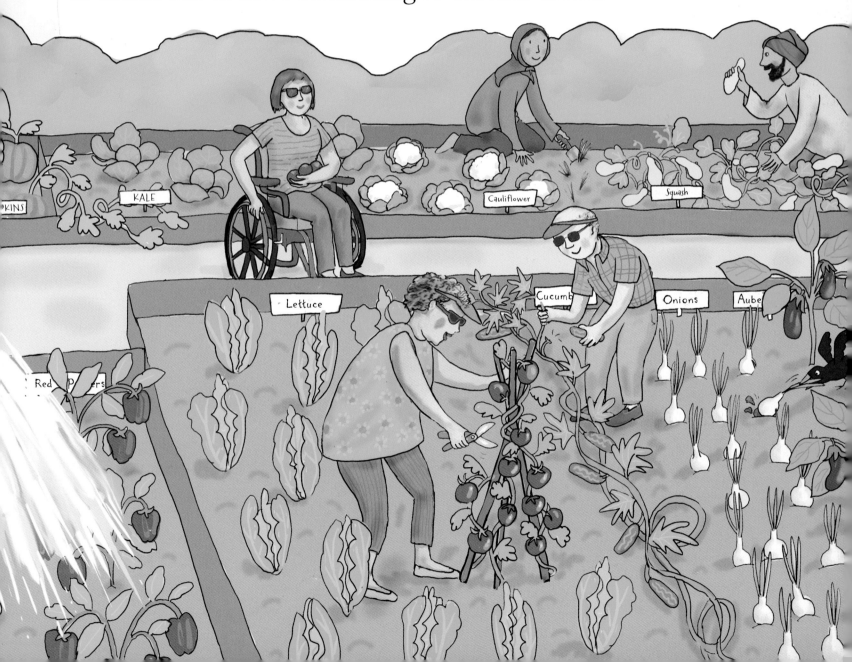

Eating many kinds of foods helps us feel healthy and good.
So each day it's important to eat plenty of vegetables and
fruit. It's also important to eat some fish, or eggs, or chicken
or other meat – or tofu, beans, peas or nuts. Some brown rice
or whole-grain breads, cereal or pasta. Some milk, yoghurt
or cheese. And just a little fat, oil and salt.

Different people and different families eat different kinds of food. Some eat all kinds of meat. Others do not eat meat that comes from cows, pigs or goats, but do eat meat that comes from chicken, turkey and fish.

I like chicken. I like tofu. And I like some veggies. So I'm glad we're cooking chicken and tofu and veggies!

Other people and families eat no meat. Instead, they eat beans, lentils, nuts or tofu to make sure they eat foods that help them grow and stay healthy. Nearly everybody eats fruit and vegetables.

I like cookies. So I'm glad we're baking cookies for our picnic!

Sometimes, between breakfast and lunch, or lunch and dinner, we feel a little hungry or tired, cranky, upset, or even angry. That's because our bodies need something to eat or drink.

If we eat a piece of fruit, or cut-up vegetables, crackers and cheese, popcorn, veggie crisps, hummus, nuts, or drink a smoothie or a glass of milk – chances are we'll feel better.

I'm a little tired and very hungry. I bet if I eat some blueberries and yoghurt or some carrots and hummus, I won't be tired or hungry anymore.

Water helps all the parts of our bodies work well. Water leaves our bodies when we wee, poo or sweat. Then we need to drink again, so that there's always water in our bodies to keep us healthy.

Water and milk are the healthiest drinks. But fruits, vegetables and even soups have water in them too. They are another way for our bodies to get the water they need.

Healthy foods and drinks do so many good things for our bodies. They help us move, breathe, think and learn new things. They give our bodies the power we need to run, jump, ride, climb, talk, laugh and play.

They help our teeth stay healthy, our muscles grow stronger and our brains and hearts work better. They help childrens' bones grow and everyone's bones stay strong. They help to stop our cuts from bleeding, to heal our broken bones, and to keep our bodies from getting sick. They help childrens' bodies grow bigger and can help all of us stay healthy.

Some kids like eating almost everything
– even new foods they've never tried before.
Others like eating only some foods and
eat the same foods again and again.
Some kids don't like any new foods.

After eating the same new food for five or six or seven or more days in a row — that food may taste good to you. And you may find out that you actually like that new food.

It's fun to eat sweet things like ice cream, a biscuit, or a piece of cake or pie, or sweets. Most sweet things have a lot of sugar in them. But too much sugar is not good for your teeth or the rest of your body.

Still, it's ok to eat some sweet things sometimes — but not too many and not too often. And they're almost always a special treat on birthdays and holidays.

Fruit and juices also have sugar in them. A lot of fruit drinks and fizzy drinks have even more sugar added. They have too much sugar in them. So it's better for your body to eat a piece of fruit and drink water than have a fruit drink or a fizzy drink.

Some kinds of foods can make some children or grown-ups feel sick and very uncomfortable. These kinds of foods may make them feel very itchy or may make them have a tummy ache. This is called having an allergy.

Nuts that grow on trees, or peanuts, or milk, or eggs, or prawns are just a few of the foods some children and grown-ups are allergic to.

This food is so yummy! And I'm not allergic to any of it. I am allergic to peanuts so I eat almond butter, not peanut butter.

Right, Gus. And there are a gazillion kinds of food that I'm not allergic to. So I can definitely eat those foods.

People who are allergic to certain foods do not eat that food. If they happen to eat food they are allergic to, they can be given medicine or an injection so that they won't get sick or feel uncomfortable from eating that food.

Some childrens' and grown-ups' stomachs can feel uncomfortable or very upset when they eat foods with wheat, barley or rye in them. They are not allergic, but they don't eat foods with wheat, barley or rye in them because these grains contain gluten. The foods they eat are called gluten-free foods.

The more we get up and move, the stronger our muscles and bones become and the better our brains work. Getting up and moving many times a day feels good. And it's fun. And it's healthy.

We also need time to rest our bodies – to look at a book, sing a song, watch a bird fly by, have a nap, or go to sleep at night. Resting our bodies is a healthy thing to do. But watching TV or playing on a computer or a phone for too long is not healthy for our bodies.

So every day, make sure you have some quiet time — some time to rest your body. Lie down on the grass, sit under a tree, or curl up with a book or someone you love. There are many wonderful ways to have quiet time.

Every day, make sure you have plenty of
time to swing your arms, kick your feet, walk, run,
ride, jump, dance, hop, skip, climb, somersault, swim — or do
whatever you like to do to make your body move. And every
day, make sure you have some time to go outside.

When you were a brand-new baby, you kicked your feet, waved your arms, moved your head from side to side, wiggled your fingers and toes, curled up, stretched, and drank breast milk or formula. When you were an older baby, you began to eat foods, roll over, and crawl. You've been eating and drinking and moving for a long time.

You know what? Eating healthy food is rrr-really good for our bodies. And so yummy!

And making sure we get up and move is rrr-really good for our bodies too. And tons of fun!

Eating healthy foods for breakfast, lunch and dinner — and healthy snacks too — helps our bodies feel good and work well. Moving our bodies — whether we wave our hands or climb a hill — also helps our bodies feel good and work well.

So every day, let's eat well and keep on moving — so that every part of our amazing bodies can stay strong and be healthy.

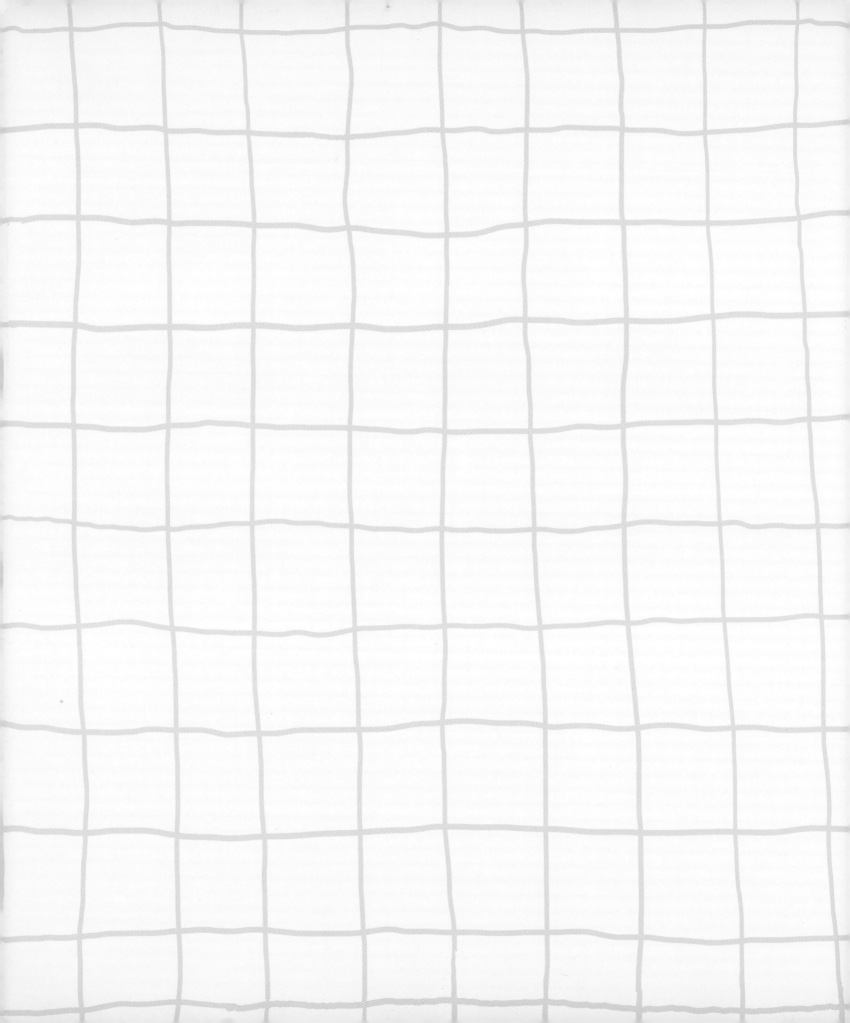